Nephi & the Plates of Brass

TEXT

Bonnie Hart Murray

ILLUSTRATIONS

Nicolle R. Murray

MUSIC

Janice Kapp Perry

The recording of
Nephi and the Plates of Brass
can be found on iTunes
and other digital download sites

Published by Hart-Murray Publishing
Aurora, Colorado

Original photos for Bonnie Hart Murray and Janice Kapp Perry
by ScottHancockPhotography.com

Music typeset by Douglas C. Perry

Printed in the United States of America

ISBN-13: 978-0-692-79840-9

ACKNOWLEDGEMENTS

I have been passionate about getting this picture book, *Nephi & the Plates of Brass,* out to the children of the Church. In writing this text, I have used 1 Nephi 3-5 as my resource, and have endeavored to fashion as many of the exact words and phrases as possible into a poetic story-form. Nearly two-thirds of the words came directly from the scriptural resources. It is my hope that this will help children to become more familiar with the phraseology of the Book of Mormon.

I have loved collaborating with so many great talents in bringing this storybook to fruition. I was thrilled with Janice's adventurous, Middle Eastern-sounding music, and it has been a special privilege to work with my sweet daughter-in-law, Nicolle, as she painted these detailed and imaginative illustrations. Many thanks to Roger Hoffman for his exciting arrangement of the music, and to Sam Payne for his special story-telling style of singing the song. Thanks also to John Perry, Janice's son and office manager, who did such a beautiful, artistic design for the book.

I would like to express gratitude for my father, Mark Hart—a writer, poet, and educator; my mother Clara Hart—loving mother of nine children; and my wonderful husband, John. Each of them provided great support and encouragement to me in the development of my talents. I would also like to express gratitude to my beloved friend and mentor Janice Kapp Perry. I can never repay her for all she has done for me. It has been a great privilege to learn about "creating" from one of the greatest composers of our church.

~Bonnie Hart Murray

To our children, our grandchildren, and our great grandchildren—and to all children everywhere. We hope you will love this adventurous, exciting, and true story about *Nephi & the Plates of Brass!*

Father Lehi dreamed a dream that they must seek the plates of brass.

Sacred writings were engraven on these records of the past.

Nephi said unto his father,
"I will do as God commands."
With his brothers, Nephi journeyed,
crossing o'er the desert sands.

As they neared the house of Laban,
keeper of the plates of brass,
lots were cast and fell on Laman;
he was chosen for the task.

When he sought the holy records
Laban thrust him out and said,
"Now behold, thou art a robber!"
From his presence Laman fled.

Lehi's sons were filled with sorrow,
but young Nephi took a stand:

"Let us now be strong and faithful,
let us keep the Lord's command!
We will gather up the riches
that our father left behind,
for he left much gold and silver;
we will trade it by design."

When they came again to Laban off'ring riches for the plates . . .

Laban sent his men to slay them,
and obtained their treasures great.

14

As they fled from Laban's servants, Laman's heart with anger stirred.

$\mathcal{h}$e and Lemuel smote their brothers,
speaking harsh and angry words.

Then an angel stood before them
and reproved them for their sin.
They must go again to Laban;
God would then deliver him.

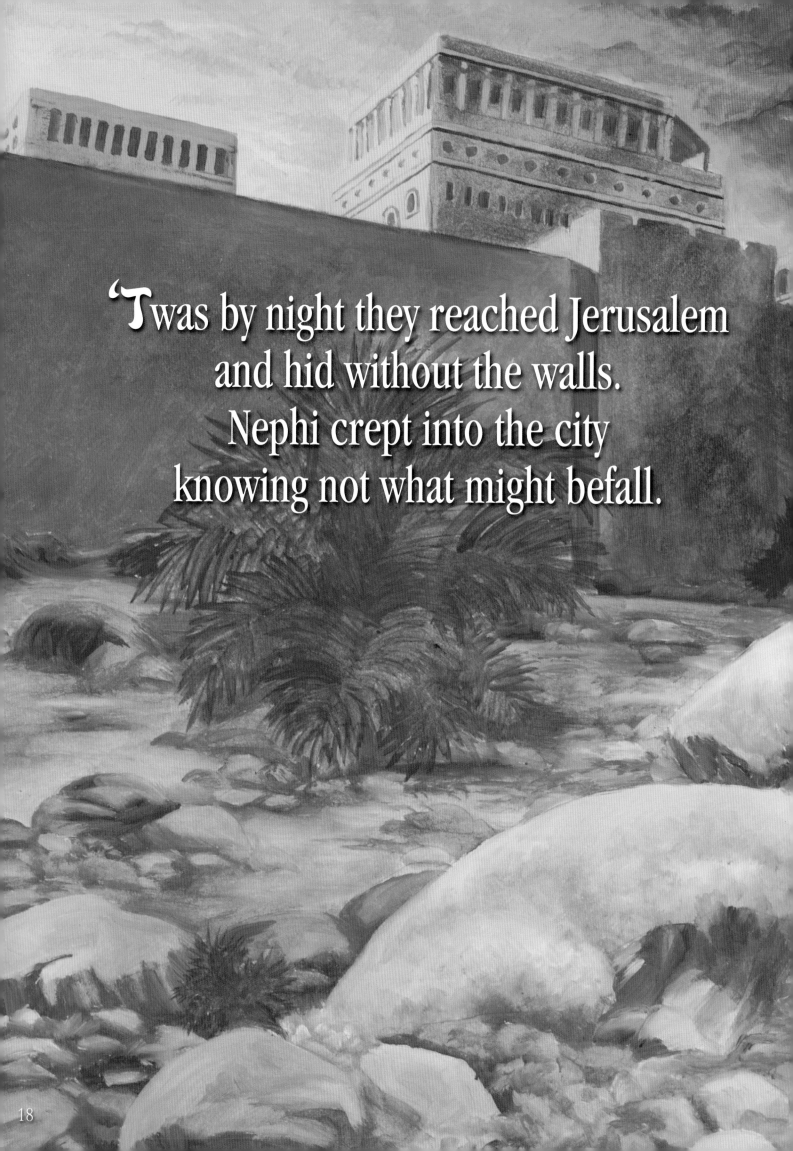

'Twas by night they reached Jerusalem
and hid without the walls.
Nephi crept into the city
knowing not what might befall.

he was led forth by the spirit,
and beheld a drunken man—
it was Laban who had fallen,
thus delivered to his hand.

He drew forth the sword of Laban,
and the hilt was of pure gold;
then he slew the wicked Laban
by commandment of the Lord.

Nephi put on Laban's garments,
with his armor and his sword.
As he went toward the treas'ry
he relied upon the Lord.

Then he saw the servant, Zoram—
keeper of the treas'ry keys.
Speaking in the voice of Laban,
he commanded, "Go with me!"

Thinking Nephi was his master,
Zoram followed after him.
Nephi then obtained the records
by the means of stratagem.

Nephi told the servant, Zoram, they must take the sacred plates to his brethren who were waiting just outside the city gates.

Knowing Laban had been mingling with the brethren of the church, wherefore Zoram followed Nephi, for he knew not whom he served.

As they came toward Nephi's brothers,
Laman and his brethren fled;
they supposed that it was Laban,
and their hearts were
filled with dread.

Nephi called out to his brethren
and they knew that it was he.
Zoram then began to tremble
and he was about to flee.

Nephi, being large in stature,
seized upon the servant there.

With an oath he spoke to Zoram,
telling him he need not fear:

"As God liveth, we will spare thee;
thou shalt have a place with us.
Go with us and be a free man!"
Nephi gained the servant's trust.

With the sacred plates they journeyed down into the wilderness.

They had kept the Lord's commandment;
generations would be blessed.

They returned to father Lehi,
and he searched the plates of brass.
This great prophet testified that
wondrous things would come to pass;

for these plates would never perish—
they would bless all men on earth—
going forth to ev'ry nation
with their message of great worth!

NEPHI & THE PLATES OF BRASS

Words by
Bonnie Hart Murray

Music by
Janice Kapp Perry

1. Fa - ther Le - hi dreamed a dream___ that they must seek the plates of brass.___ Sa - cred
(2. When they) came a - gain to La - ban, off'- ring rich - es for the plates,___ La - ban
(3. Ne - phi) put on La - ban's gar - ments, with his ar - mor and his sword. As he
(4. Ne - phi) called out to his breth - ren and they knew that it was he.___ Zo - ram

writ - ings were en - grav - en on these rec - ords of the past.___ Ne - phi
sent his men to slay___ them, and ob - tained their treas - ures great.___ As they
went to - ward the treas - 'ry he re - lied up - on the Lord.___ Then he
then be - gan to trem - ble, and he was a - bout to flee.___ Ne - phi,

said un - to his fa - ther, "I will do as God com - mands."_ With his
fled from La - ban's ser - vants, La - man's heart with an - ger stirred.___ He and
saw the ser - vant, Zo - ram, keep - er of the trea - s'ry keys.___ Speak - ing
be - ing large in stat - ure, seized up - on the ser - vant there.___ With an

broth - ers, Ne - phi jour - neyed, cross - ing o'er the des - ert sands.
Lem - uel smote their broth - ers, speak - ing harsh and an - gry words.
in the voice of La - ban, he com - mand - ed, "Go with me!"
oath he spoke to Zo - ram tell - ing him he need not fear:

As they neared the house of La - ban, keep - er
Then an an - gel stood be - fore them and re -
Think - ing Ne - phi was his mas - ter, Zo - ram

"As God liv - eth, we will spare thee; thou shalt

Vs. 2 & 4
ten.

of the plates of brass, lots were cast and fell on La - man; he was
proved them for their sin. They must go a - gain to La - ban; God would
fol - lowed af - ter him. Ne - phi then ob - tained the rec - ords by the
have a place with us; Go with us and be a free - man!" Ne - phi

cho - sen for the task. When he sought the ho - ly rec - ords La - ban
then de - liv - er him. 'Twas by night they reached Je - ru - sa - lem and
means of stra - ta - gem. Ne - phi told the ser - vant, Zo - ram, they must
gained the ser - vant's trust. With the sa - cred plates they jour - neyed down in -

Slower ♩ = 52

ten. **A tempo** ♩ = 63

thrust him out and said, "Now be - hold, thou art a rob - ber!" From His
hid with - out the walls. Ne - phi crept in - to the cit - y know - ing
take the sa - cred plates to his breth - ren who were wait - ing just out-
to the wil - der - ness. They had kept the Lord's com - mand - ment; gen - e -

pres - ence La - man fled. Le - hi's
not what might be - fall. He was
side the cit - y gates. Know - ing
ra - tions would be blessed. They re -

sons were filled with sor - row, but young Ne - phi took a stand: "Let us
led forth by the spir - it, and be - held a drunk - en man— it was
La - ban had been ming - ling with the breth - ren of the church, where - fore,
turned to Fa - ther Le - hi, and he searched the plates of brass. This great

now be strong and faith - ful, let us keep the Lord's com - mand! We will
La - ban who had fal - len, thus de - liv - ered to his hand. He drew
Zo - ram fol - lowed Ne - phi, for he knew not whom he served. As they
proph - et tes - ti - fied that won - drous things would come to pass; for these

40

gath - er up the rich - es that our fa - ther left be - hind, for he
forth the sword of La - ban, and the hilt was of pure gold; then he
came toward Ne - phi's broth - ers, La - man and his breth - ren fled; they sup -
plates would ne - ver per - ish— they would bless all men on earth— go - ing

25

Opt. v. 4 |1.2.3.| A tempo ♩ = 63

left much gold and sil - ver; we will trade it by de - sign." 2. When they
slew the wick - ed La - ban by com - mand - ment of the Lord. 3. Ne - phi
posed that it was La - ban, and their hearts were filled with dread. 4. Ne - phi
forth to ev -'ry na - tion, with their

f   *poco rit.*   *mf*

A tempo ♩ = 63

27

|4. *rit.*

mes - sage of great worth!

rit.   *f*   *rit.*

30

ARTIST BIOS

Bonnie Hart Murray attended Brigham Young University for two years, then later graduated magna cum laude from Metropolitan University of Denver at the age of sixty with a bachelor of art degree in music and a piano emphasis. Bonnie and Janice Kapp Perry have collaborated on several Book of Mormon projects. They have written 28 Book of Mormon hymns together. This collection of hymns was recently published next to the artwork of Tom Lovell, as well as the complete Book of Mormon art collection by Arnold Friberg, in a beautiful keepsake volume called *A Songbook for LDS Families*. They also produced a CD and songbook/program entitled *The Book of Mormon Has Come Forth*, orchestrated by Merrill Jenson and recorded by the City of Prague Philharmonic Orchestra in the Czech Republic. Bonnie and her husband, John, have six children, eleven grandchildren, and one great-grandchild. They live in Aurora, Colorado.

Nicolle R. Murray is a freelance illustrator specializing in children's books. She graduated from BYU-Idaho in 2004 with a Bachelors Degree in Graphic Design and Illustration with a minor in History. Since that time she has avidly illustrated books, designed graphics, painted fine art, played around in multimedia and 3D projects all the while maintaining her love of books, gardening, cooking, learning, and 'getting her hands into' other creative-type pursuits. Her favorite use of time, besides art, is spending time with her husband Adam. (www.facebook.com/caperingcastles)

Janice Kapp Perry received her musical training at Brigham Young University and has been writing and recording gospel music for forty years. She composed *As Sisters In Zion* for the LDS hymnbook and ten songs that are in the *Children's Songbook*. She has recorded more than eighty albums of gospel music, written 250 hymns, and composed music for two full-length musicals. Janice sang with the Mormon Tabernacle Choir in the 1990's and the choir has sung and recorded several of her songs. She received the Exemplary Woman Award from Ricks College in 1994, and BYU's Distinguished Alumni Award in 1997. In 2001 she received the Lifetime Achievement Award from the Faith Centered Music Association. In 2009 BYU Broadcasting filmed a sixty-minute documentary of her life entitled *Janice Kapp Perry: A Lifetime of Service and Song*. Janice and her husband, Douglas, served a full-time mission to Santiago, Chile. They live in Provo, Utah, near their four children, thirteen grandchildren, and seven great-grandchildren.